Savannah Sketchbook

The author gratefully acknowledges Paula S. Wallace, President of the Savannah College of Art and Design, whose vision inspired the creation of *Savannah Sketchbook*.

Special thanks to the following individuals for their assistance in making *Savannah Sketchbook* possible:
Professor Sandra Reed, Professor Josh Yu, student artists of the Savannah College of Art and Design, Janice Shay, Winslett Long, Mark Rand, Elizabeth Hudson-Goff, Venessa Austin Price Sylvester, Margaret Wayt DeBolt, Gloria Underwood and Pamela Afifi

Cover art by Heng-Ching Chang
Design by Janice Shay

Published in cooperation with Community Communications, Inc.
4520 Executive Park Drive, Montgomery, Alabama 36116

Printed in Canada
10 9 8 7 6 5 4 3 2

2nd printing 2001

Library of Congress Catalog number: 00-056992
ISBN 1-58192-019-9

The Middle Georgia Art Association

*Inspiring the creativity, imagination and talent of Macon
artists, young and old, for more than 30 years*

rt for art's sake is not just an idyllic concept at the Middle Georgia Art Association; it's a fact of everyday life that has enriched the lives of Macon residents for almost 40 years.

A non-profit organization dedicated to the promotion of the visual arts in middle Georgia, the association sponsors exhibits, festivals, art classes, scholarships and other programs for its members and the general community. Its working gallery regularly displays the works of its members and sponsors several invitational exhibits by non-member artists whose work merits community support, such as the annual exhibit held on behalf of Georgia Artists with Disabilities.

Founded in the 1960s by local artists including graduates of Wesleyan College and Mercer University, the association was at first a means by which these colleagues could continue to gather and create art together. The association's first meeting place was the Hay House, a Macon landmark dating back to the Civil War era.

Today, the current membership includes more than 450 artists, ranging from eight to 90 years of age. The association's exhibit gallery and administrative offices are located in Payne Mill Village, Macon, where its principal staff are also experienced artists themselves.

Beth Stewart, Ph.D., president of the association, holds a doctorate in art history and is the current chair of Mercer University's Art Department.

Charlotte Beeler, the association's gallery director, specializes in drawing, painting and three-dimensional art, while Patty Bradley, the association's office manager, is also a water colorist. Both women also teach art courses at the facility. "I think art is extremely important as a whole, no matter what facet of it you're talking about," Bradley commented. "Art, whether it's visual art, music or theatre, is invaluable to the community. I find it very encouraging that more and more parents appreciate the value of art in their children's education."

Creativity is contagious, Bradley also pointed out, explaining that this is why so many amateur and professional artists find coming to the association so stimulating.

It's also affordable. With adult memberships only $20 a year, student memberships just $10 a year and annual family memberships a mere $25, it's no wonder why the Middle Georgia Art Association is so popular among its members, no matter what their social, economic or cultural background.

But affordability is far from all that the association offers. Scholarships for art lessons are available for deserving high school and middle school students, as well as an annual college-level art exhibition that offers prize money that can be applied toward further education. There's even a summer art camp for younger students.

The association also features workshops in which well-known artists participate, guest speakers who present programs at monthly meetings and special exhibits on different fields of classic and contemporary art, such as digital photography.

Funded in large part by private donations and the proceeds from the annual Mulberry Street Arts Festival held in Macon during the two-day March Cherry Blossom Festival, the Middle Georgia Art Association continues to thrive.

Like the artistic creations of its members, The Middle Georgia Art Association proves, with each new generation, that it is truly the heart of this state's finest "work in progress." ∎

The Middle Georgia Art Association

The Middle Georgia Art Association is located at 342 Rose Avenue, Payne Mill Village, Macon, Ga. Gallery hours, Monday through Saturday, are between 11 a.m. and 5:30 p.m.

For more information about exhibits or how to become a member, please contact Patty Bradley or Charlotte Beeler at (478) 744-9557, or at mgart@juno.com.

Savannah Sketchbook

FOREWORD BY TONY BENNETT

TEXT BY JEFFREY ELEY

ILLUSTRATIONS BY ARTISTS OF THE
SAVANNAH COLLEGE OF ART AND DESIGN

DESIGN PRESS
A Division of the Savannah College of Art and Design

Contents

The Artists

Students in the *Savannah
Sketchbook* scholarship
painting class.

BACK
Chang-Hyun Kim
Jean Lim
Linda Rorer
Aaron Crayne
Sumiyo Toribe
Robin Reynolds
Jon Wink

MIDDLE
Professor Sandra Reed
Heng-Ching Chang
Sarah Alexander
Christopher Hoff
Jonathan Newsome
Wempy Homeric

FRONT
Charul Sakultanapaisal
Lin Wang
Jo-Shan Ma
Dana Sink
Steven Johnson
Andrew Holahan
Brian Main

Tony Bennett

One of the great benefits of being a musical performer is that through concert touring you end up becoming a world citizen. For fifty years I have traveled all over the globe and have visited every major city in the U.S. at least once. And as an artist, I have painted the views and landscapes of most of them. Savannah remains one of my favorites because it is a city built and maintained with great care. It is a city that has preserved and respected its past while still accepting the necessary changes that occur with the passing of time. Savannah reminds me of a great song, finely crafted by a composer—such as Savannah's own, Johnny Mercer—that is turned over to a singer who adds his own personal statement. The citizens of Savannah have done just that, and, as a result, have enlivened this place, filling it with genuine charm and unique character.

It is little wonder that Savannah has encouraged so many artists to capture its beauty and grace. From the pastels of its gardens to the auburn of its brickwork, Savannah radiates without overpowering, requiring a palette that softens and glows. This is the challenge of painting landscapes that is so exciting and provoking—determining the special strength and soul of each place that makes it different from all the rest. Each city has its own secrets and mystery.

Savannah is no different. The paintings and drawings reproduced in this singular volume reflect the absorption and passion these artists have felt in rendering their subject. It is done with affection and love, expressing the beauty and innate worth of a "place." The works in *Savannah Sketchbook* convey exactly what they should—whether through a quick sketch or studied rendition—impressions of unique and uplifting experiences. I am pleased to contribute my own watercolor of a Savannah scene to the *Sketchbook* as I, too, was inspired by the city's beauty. *Savannah Sketchbook* captures the city's most endearing qualities and allows us to revisit this wonderful place again and again.

Jean Lim

A stroll through Savannah enables one to glimpse its array of spectacular architecture. These buildings tell stories of Savannah's rich history.

Even the original trustees of the colony could not have predicted that Savannah would evolve into one of the most charming, romantic, and historically important cities in America. While many Europeans in the eighteenth century saw colonial expansion as a means to secure greater power and prestige, others envisioned the opportunity to create ideal communities founded in shared philosophies and goals. General James Edward Oglethorpe believed all this was possible as he headed the settlement of this thirteenth, and last, British colony in North America. A decorated military leader and member of the British House of Commons, Oglethorpe became the most instrumental individual in the development of Georgia—named for the reigning King, George II.

His government agreed to aid the development of the colony for several reasons. To the north, South Carolina was immensely prosperous with a wealth virtually unparalleled by any other colony except Virginia. To the south were the expansionist interests of the Spanish in Florida, and Oglethorpe was charged with establishing a colony that would buffer the two.

As in South Carolina, the trustees of the Georgia colony believed it could be very lucrative. Prior to the founding, there was optimism that the area would be suitable for silk and wine production. Although these did not prove successful, rice farming was established during the eighteenth century and remained the principal crop. Eventually, it was abandoned, as cotton became more profitable. Also, the rice fields were notorious breeding sites of mosquitoes that contributed to several devastating outbreaks of yellow fever during the colony's first one hundred years. Consequently, with the lack of a successful economic focus, Georgia ranked as the poorest of the original colonies.

However, Oglethorpe believed his colony could achieve more than simply the protection of rich planters near Charleston and profit for the trustees. He saw social opportunity. London's streets were filled with countless unemployed and English prisons were overcrowded with debtors. Like many others in Parliament, Oglethorpe was distressed about the way the British legal system handled the circumstances of the poor. Prison conditions were horrendous and many men were imprisoned with little ability to correct their situation. Significantly, a friend of Oglethorpe, author and architect Robert Castell, had died in jail unable to pay his debts.

Oglethorpe believed he could bring positive change to his settlers with the development of a program of hard work and temperance. Oglethorpe's colony abolished drinking. (Some Savannahians still believe this is why most of the early settlers moved to South Carolina.) Nevertheless, this principle appealed to many of the early colonists that came to Savannah in pursuit of greater religious freedom. In fact, these individuals represent a larger number of early settlers to the colony than debtors.

THE PLAN

Oglethorpe selected Yamacraw Bluff, the location of the colony's first settlement, for its geographic advantages. Named for the river, Savannah was far enough upriver to enjoy greater security from possible Spanish attack by sea or plunder by pirate ships. The settlement was high, expansive, and suitable for the creation of a community of buildings. Farming plots were also part of the early program for the colony and kept small because slavery, like alcohol, was initially prohibited. This ban helped to eliminate the concern that slaves would serve as allies to any enemy that might invade. Originally, Savannah was to be surrounded by a fortress palisade. This proved unnecessary, as the local Yamacraw people, native the area, were friendly to the new settlers.

The plan for Savannah combined a practical organization with rules and regulations that reflected the hopes for the new colony. Grid-like, the city plan covered a large rectangle

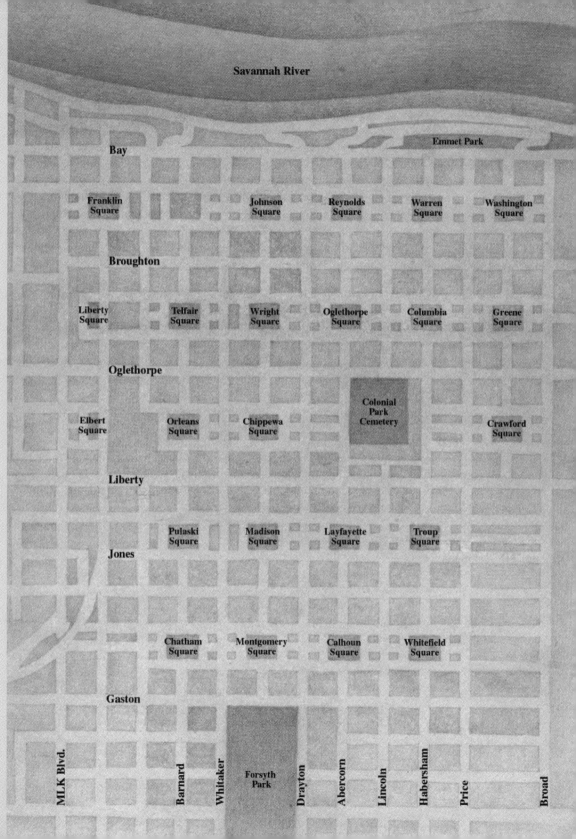

The Plan

Chang-Hyun Kim

Savannah is one of America's true urban treasures. Her citizens recognize and honor this through ensuring the continuation of its beauty and integrity.

a little less than one-half mile parallel to the Savannah River reaching just ove one-quarter mile inland. The bluff was divided into six equal units, called ward Each ward had four tithings with ten lots that were intended to handle forty free holder families. Additionally, each ward had four trust lots that were designate for important public buildings like churches and storehouses.

The plan included a large open area in the center of each ward. These space were originally intended to serve many functions—from training ground for th military to grazing room for cattle. They represent the most significant an enduring element of Oglethorpe's planned community. Today these spaces ar called "squares" and their appearance is not much different from what yo would have seen one or two hundred years ago. More than a positive answer t the cramped disorder of many European communities, the squares combine the virtue of nature into the rigid, careful plan that Oglethorpe established.

The plan for Savannah was determined, at least in part, before the firs colonists left England, and the grid reflects some of the emerging scientific an mathematical theories which were being applied to contemporary life in the earl eighteenth century. Although no specific precedent can be pointed to, there are ear lier urban plans with interesting parallels to the plan established by Oglethorpe.

Undoubtedly, books provided Oglethorpe with ideas for the first settle ment in the new colony. Since antiquity, many towns had grown from grid-lik patterns, as the Greeks and the Romans preferred to arrange their communi ties in this fashion. Oglethorpe owned a copy of *The Villas of the Ancients* which was authored by his friend Castell before he went to prison. Castell wa part of the Palladian circle led by Lord Burlington, and their appreciation fo Vitruvius and the order of Roman architecture and planning is highlighted i Castell's book.

Of course, contemporary developments in London town planning wer important to Oglethorpe, and during the seventeenth and eighteenth centurie London saw the development of several squares. Earliest, and possibly most sig nificant, was Covent Garden. Inspired by Italian piazzas and the Place de Vosges in Paris, Inigo Jones' design for Covent Garden drew from Palladia concepts that communities have formal, open spaces for necessary activitie Oglethorpe's admiration for this design feature suggests some influence on th prominent incorporation of similar spaces in Savannah's plan.

Inspiration may be traced as far away as China. Through travel book Western Europeans were becoming more aware of Asian cultures and communi ties. In particular, several historians have noted interesting similarities between the patterns of Savannah's squares and streets and those of Beijing.

Oglethorpe's military background included a deep appreciation for military science and architecture. He was familiar with writings on fortification and fortification design. Many Italian works of the later sixteenth and seventeenth centuries illustrate proposals and plans that have interesting similarities to Savannah. In addition, seventeenth century plans for several English military outposts and colonial towns in Northern Ireland include regular grid plans. Established in part to help relocate many families in poverty, the colonial settlement of Londonderry was planned with a grid of streets and squares.

Notwithstanding, the grid must have been seen as the most efficient and effective way to apportion property to the new settlers. This had happened to different degrees in each of the colonies. Savannah was not the first planned community in British North America, as it is often reported. Several other communities had been planned, and some of the most famous having grid components include New Haven, Connecticut; Philadelphia, Pennsylvania; Annapolis, Maryland; and Williamsburg, Virginia. However, Savannah's plan is most significant.

Jo-Shan Ma

Monuments and elegant fountains have replaced the fire towers and wandering livestock of bygone years, but Savannah's squares remain vivid examples of the city's original plan.

Sarah Alexander

The Telfair mansion, designed by William Jay, was christened the Telfair Academy of Arts and Sciences in 1875. As Savannah's oldest art museum, the Telfair maintains its role as a leader in the Savannah art community.

COLONIAL SAVANNAH

The first houses were extremely modest and measured approximately 24 by 16 feet with a sleeping loft under a simple gable roof. None of these original buildings survives. Nor does Savannah retain any trace of the Yamacraw settlement, and very little specific information has been uncovered about the way the first African Americans lived after slavery was permitted around mid-century.

Beyond the initial six wards, to the southeast of the community, the original settlers established their cemetery. Further to the south, the colony was divided into a series of five-acre plots. Beyond those were forty-acre farms. Mid-eighteenth century maps survive that illustrate these divisions and include delightful title blocks with surrounding reference to the farming tools used by the first Georgians.

Savannah grew slowly throughout the eighteenth century as many early colonists elected to travel inland or northward. For most of the Revolutionary War, the town was under the rule of the British, who had secured control of the small port in 1778 and defeated a colonial force that tried to recapture it in 1779. The Battle of Savannah was a devastating defeat for the American army with upwards of one thousand casualties. British forces would not relinquish Savannah until 1782, several months after Lord Cornwallis surrendered to General George Washington at Yorktown.

When President Washington visited Savannah in 1791, he found a city of mostly modest wooden structures. However, the early houses, churches and taverns were beginning to clearly define the streets and squares of the plan. Few eighteenth century buildings survive because of the first of several ruinous fires which occurred during Savannah's history. In 1796, an enormous blaze destroyed two-thirds of the buildings Washington might have seen.

WHEN COTTON WAS KING

The port grew rapidly after the turn of the century and the success of the cotton gin quickly established Savannah as the preeminent cotton port on the Atlantic coast. Shipping between the city and destinations in England and New England clogged the wharves and riverfront with handsome sailing ships and, later in the

The 1821 residence built for Isaiah Davenport blends elements of Georgian and Neoclassical style. When it was threatened with demolition in the 1950s, the Davenport House was a catalyst for the creation of the Historic Savannah Foundation.

On sultry summer afternoons, the shade of live oaks is akin to heaven for Savannahians, who have traditionally viewed the squares as extensions of their homes.

When Cotton Was King

century, steam-powered vessels.

Before 1820, Savannah had begun to displa its new wealth with architectural embellish ments that rivaled many towns and cities i America. Culturally, most American ports alon the Atlantic Ocean remained indebted to th trends and fashions of Great Britain. Savanna was no different, as best illustrated by the contri butions of the English-born architect Willia Jay. Although his public work has bee destroyed or greatly altered, several of hi domestic designs still stand as testimony t Savannah's initial nineteenth century prosperit

Regency England was consumed in it romance with classicism. Jay's houses are th finest American examples of this elegant ag Dominated by elements identified as Gree Revival, his buildings were creative an dynamic. Although he never traveled t Greece, "quoting" antique architecture was th hallmark of good design and often seen as a acknowledgment of the classical education both the architect and owner. In addition t style, they were modern in their construction For example, recent archaeology has deter mined that Jay employed extremely sophisticat ed and advanced systems of plumbing and cool ing in his Savannah homes.

Jay's exteriors were monumental in an oth erwise mostly frame community. Evocative the rational and stylized approaches of Sir Joh Soane, Jay had an eagerness to please his client through the use of powerful, symmetrical, an handsome exteriors adorned with correct clas sical embellishments. Likewise, Jay's interior were as elegant as they were imposing, clearl intended to impress any visitor to the home. Jay delighted in the opportunity to dazzle the guest by producing sumptuous entrance halls often dominated by the combined features of columns and elaborate staircases.

Of the four residences attributed to Jay, one was demolished in the early twentieth century, two have been altered, and one survives essentially unchanged since the 1830s. Extensive alterations that reflected a variety of uses all but destroyed the interiors of Jay's Scarbrough residence. However, recent restorations have returned many original elements, including a dramatic skylit atrium-like entrance hall. For the Telfair family, Jay borrowed similar Greek forms and elements as he did for William Scarbrough. Converted to a museum in the late nineteenth century, the Telfair retains elements of Jay's original design. Most interesting are the entrance porch that features beautiful Corinthian columns and the Roman thermae window that rises above the porch entablature.

Gone, sadly, is the house that Jay built for the Bulloch family in 1820. Surviving images illustrate that it was a solid, dignified salute to the antique with proportions similar to those seen in his design for the Telfair mansion. Of Jay's magical entrance halls, this was probably the finest, as it included a circular staircase surrounded by six Corinthian columns.

Jay arrived in Savannah in 1817, and it is Jay's first residential design that is least altered and considered the premier example of Savannah's Regency style architecture. Designed for the brother-in-law of William Jay's sister, Anne, the Richardson-Owens-Thomas House was completed in 1819.

Jay built the house using a mixture of materials. Most famous, and most important, were tabby and coquina. The entrance portico on this home is lighter in scale than his later works and the ionic columns are more delicate. The side porch is a tour-de-force of cast iron classical elements.

Exciting features on the interior include the only surviving Jay staircase. The unusual design includes a bridge that gives access to the chambers at the rear of the upper floor. This bridge is arched to provide additional headroom at the landing level and is illuminated by colored glass lights from the upstairs hall.

Equally intriguing features are found in the parlor and dining room. Seemingly inspired by the shallow dome and vaulted spaces found in Soane's English work, Jay suggests a similar feel in the formal parlor. The dining room utilizes a brilliant mixture of concave and convex shapes with an amber glass light decorated boldly and simply with a Greek key. As historians have noted, one wonders how Jay was able to educate, maybe even convince, the local builders to execute such unusual design elements.

When Jay departed in 1821, Savannah was in the throes of recession. Yellow fever had ravaged the city the previous year, the port had been closed, and cotton prices were down. A second devastating fire had consumed many buildings, and the mood of the citizens that greeted Jay four years earlier had changed dramatically. It would take a decade, but by the early 1830s Savannah had reestablished its momentum and during the next thirty years, would witness its most important contributions to American history.

As Savannah grew, the original arrangement of wards with central squares was continued. The squares provided open spaces for citizens and visitors and, during the first half of the nineteenth century, most of those in the more prominent wards were being landscaped into small parks. Many were fenced to eliminate carts and carriages from driving straight through. Several were decorated with important antebellum monuments. Most notable were those placed in some of the squares on Bull Street, including the obelisk in Johnson Square that honors Revolutionary War hero Nathanael Greene.

As they evolved into places more decorative and less utilitarian, the squares became popular spaces for socializing. During the nineteenth and earlier twentieth centuries, many Savannahians considered them as outdoor living rooms. Although the comforts of air conditioning have diminished their appeal during the long summers, squares still function as favorite places for weddings, reunions and other celebrations.

Savannah boasts some of America's most extraordinary examples of wrought and cast iron decorative details, often overlooked by a passserby.

Charul Sakultanapaisal

When Cotton Was King

Greek Revivalism dominated domestic design in American architectu during the first half of the nineteenth century. In Savannah, one of the notab architects after Jay to favor this style was the Irish-born Charles Cluskey. H arrived in 1838 and, over the next ten years, produced several city mansions a numerous row houses dominated by Greek-inspired elements. His design f the home of Francis Sorrel on Madison Square and his possible contributio to the monumental Aaron Champion House on Orleans Square are significa examples.

However, it is Cluskey's design of numerous row houses, and those similar them, that began to truly define most of Savannah's streets before 185 Aesthetically, Greek Revivalism prevailed. As the city expanded, tithings we being filled with double houses and row houses. For fire safety, most of these we of brick, many were covered with stucco, and some projects by Cluskey and ot ers would stretch the entire block. One of the most interesting examples can st be seen near what was the southern edge of the city at the beginning of the Civ War. Now referred to as Gordon Row, these buildings and others like the housed Savannah's growing middle class during this era of prosperity.

By the 1850s, the population of Savannah was nearly twenty thousand a Oglethorpe's plan had been repeated to include twenty-four wards. In the spir of Central Park, Savannah developed Forsyth Park. Located at the end of Bu Street on the southern edge of the city, the park served as both a parade grour for soldiers and a gathering space for citizens. Forsyth Park was immediate popular, and Savannah's most beautiful fountain was installed there in 185 During that same decade, a Swedish visitor, writer Frederika Bremer, note "There cannot be a more beautiful city in the world."

The Central of Georgia Railroad selected Savannah as the terminus for o of the South's most developed rail systems, and warehouses built along the rive front were filled to the rafters with cotton from upcountry plantations. Toda these warehouses represent an extremely important assemblage of surviving nin teenth century commercial and industrial architecture. Many of these building are still reached from the Bay Street side by iron bridges that span the bumpy col blestone ramps that travel down to the river. These bridges, called "Facto Walks," are named for the cotton brokers who determined prices and, in sever instances, made millions.

In the decade before the Civil War, Savannah had become one of the South leading cities. Only Charleston, New Orleans and Richmond were as large c famous. The 1850s saw Savannah preoccupied with cotton. One visitor wrote, "It was cotton in the morning, cotton at noon, and cotton in the evening." The importance of the port of Savannah at this time is best reflected in the imposing Greek Revival Customs House. Standing at the southeast corner of Bay Street and Bull Street, it was designed by New York architect John Norris. This handsome Greek Revival building was completed in 1852 and demonstrated a level of professionalism and ability that would attract many of the city's wealthiest families to contract with Norris to design their homes.

For cotton broker Andrew Low, Norris produced an exceptional town home in the Greek style. Although declining in popularity by the 1840s, Greek Revivalism retained a strong appeal in the American South until the Civil War. The Andrew Low House is embellished with some of the finest neo-classical detailing and interiors of the period. Only the extension of eaves and addition of bracket supports hint to the rising romanticism for Italianate forms.

Norris designed other notable houses during the 1850s, and their styles reflect the growing eclecticism seen in mid-nineteenth century architecture. Of these, it is on Madison Square that he completed his Savannah masterpiece. Erected at a cost of one hundred thousand dollars, the home built for Charles Green was Savannah's most expensive and is one of the finest examples of Gothic Revival domestic architecture in America. Emphasizing elements from the Tudor period, the Green-Meldrim house, as it is known today, was coated in stucco and scored to look like stone. This provided a closer imitation of distant castles that inspired its romantic design.

Green, like Low, had made a fortune in the cotton trade and could afford to include in his home the most modern conveniences and elaborate decorations available. The fact that Union General William Tecumsah Sherman selected this residence for his Savannah lodging during the famous Civil War "March to the Sea" across Georgia suggests that he found it to be the finest available.

Entrance to the home is gained by passing under a magnificent ironwork porch of medieval inspiration and through a triple set of double doors into a broad hall that runs the entire depth of the house. Tiled, it separates generous parlors on one side from two slightly smaller rooms and a beautiful sweeping stair on the opposite side. Original to the house, but from different periods of the nineteenth century, are the hallway consoles and the imported mirrors in the parlors.

However, Savannah was not only a city of well-to-do planters and merchants. By contrast, laborers lived in modest homes on the eastern and western fringes of the city. Few survive, save some pre-Civil War workers' housing in the area to the east of Price Street. Known today as the Beach Institute neighborhood, this district became a popular area for freed African-Americans who found jobs working with the railroads, on the riverfront or as domestics in the larger residences closer to Bull Street. Until the early twentieth century, African-American families continued to erect small homes on a scale similar to those first buildings erected by Oglethorpe.

AFTER THE WAR

By the outbreak of the Civil War, the population of the city had risen to twenty-three thousand. As with other Southern towns and cities, the Civil War proved disastrous to antebellum Savannah — both to her psyche and economy. Many families had lost fathers and brothers to the "cause," and the fortunes of most citizens had been greatly diminished or totally wiped out. Long overdue, freedom created a new and undefined status among African-Americans and, combined with economic instability, led to a period of chaos.

Because the city was filled to the rafters with cotton, Savannah was spared the horrible fate of other Southern communities such as Atlanta, Columbia, South Carolina and Richmond, Virginia. Trading at pennies per pound before the war, the value of cotton had risen to almost two dollars a pound by 1864. Calculated by Sherman to be worth over ten million dollars, the cotton was far too precious to destroy. In December of 1864, Sherman wrote to President Lincoln: "I beg to present you as Christmas Gift, the City of Savannah with 150 heavy guns and plenty of ammunition; and also about twenty-five thousand bales of cotton."

Relieved at her good fortune in avoiding Sherman's torch, Savannah quickly regained the prominence she had enjoyed and by the early 1870s the port was filled with ships. New warehouses had been constructed along the riverfront, and the mood was optimistic. Undoubtedly, this is due in part to the fact that after the surrender of the city, but before the surrender of the Confederacy at Appomatox, Savannah merchants had already positioned themselves to re-establish their cotton businesses.

Once again, cotton was Savannah's king, and the Savannah Cotton Exchange, erected during this period, confirmed the city's return to the world stage. New family fortunes were made; old fortunes re-emerged or were regained. The pre-war building boom returned, and the city began to exhibit more modern urban features. Streets began to be paved, more effective drainage systems were installed and the first streetcars appeared. So did the first suburbs.

During the 1870s, Savannah embraced the growing popularity of the French-inspired style of the Second Empire. The residence built for Alderman S. P. Hamilton in the early 1870s initiated the enthusiasm, followed by several other homes in the city. Mansard roofs were even added to enlarge

and "modernize" some of the stately Greek Revival residences. The most notab[le] example tops the Champion residence facing Orleans Square.

As the city expanded southward to the east and west of Forsyth Park, suburba[n] neighborhoods reflected Victorian influence. Dominated by buildings enhanced wit[h] flamboyant ornament, these Victorian neighborhoods were eventually dotted wi[th] many fine homes. Wooden homes became more prevalent as the cost of lumber in th[e] later nineteenth century declined dramatically. Although most of these houses sold f[or] thirty-five hundred dollars or less, some featured remarkable towers and oth[er] elaborate embellishments. Wonderful and inexpensive decorative "gingerbrea[d]" contributed to the popularity of large porches and verandas for outdoor living an[d] entertaining. Fine examples stand on Gaston Street near Whitefield Squar[e]. Other styles followed the lead of H.H. Richardson's inventive Romanesque-influ[u]enced architectural notions and the popular Queen Anne tastes of the English.

The most interesting buildings built during this period were by the Bosto[n] based architect William Gibbons Preston. Influenced by Richardson's love [of] medieval details, romantic silhouettes and careful craftsmanship, Preston was [to] oversee the design and construction of several important works in the late 1880[s] the Savannah Cotton Exchange, the DeSoto Hotel (sadly demolished in 1968[)] and the new county courthouse. At the same time, he designed and enlarged sev[eral] residences. Most significant of these is the home he built for his college frien[d] George Baldwin. From the broad round arches of the front porch to the delight[ful] ful Dutch gable overlooking the garden, this house, when completed in 1888, wa[s] probably the most modern in the city.

Most of the Preston-designed buildings featured a mix of brick and terra cott[a] with an emphasis on texture and visual delight. In 1892 his castle-like armory f[or] the Savannah Volunteer Guards was nearly completed on the southeastern edg[e] of Madison Square and complemented his monumental hotel building across th[e] way. However, it is his magnificent cotton-inspired decoration in terra cotta o[n] the southern facade of the Cotton Exchange on Bay Street and the brilliant towe[r] on the Courthouse facing Wright Square that represent his most unusual an[d] important architectural details. With this tower, Preston contributed an unprece[e]dented feature that seemed to anticipate Art Nouveau, animating the charmin[g] city skyline already dominated by a multitude of church spires. From the towe[r] one can still look southwest and see Savannah's most glorious steeple rising hig[h] above Independent Presbyterian Church.

As the nineteenth century drew to a close, Savannah could boast a wealth [of] religious architecture that matched the city's most notable public buildings and private residences. Collectively, these buildings represent the denominational diversity of the city and one of America's most beautiful urban concentrations of churches, cathedrals and synagogues. Like Plymouth Rock, Savannah served as a refuge for those seeking religious tolerance, and the original trustees recognized they could be instrumental in settling the colony. Within the first decades, Jews, Salzburgers and Moravians were settling alongside Presbyterians, Methodists, Baptists, and Anglicans.

As directed by Oglethorpe's town plan, many houses of worship have been located on trust lots throughout most wards, and some wards still have two or more active churches. In design, the buildings erected before and after the Civil War reflected the popular styles of the period. Notable Greek- and Roman-inspired designs are evident in Christ Episcopal Church, Trinity Methodist Church and First African Baptist Church—erected by free blacks before the Civil War. After mid-century, Gothic Revivalism dominated the design of Savannah's new religious architecture. At this time, some existing temple-form church buildings, such as the Lutheran Church of the Ascension, were remodeled to display the more fashionable medieval styles.

The earliest church to feature Gothic elements prominently was St. John's Episcopal on Madison Square. The church was built in the 1850s to the plans of Calvin Otis, an architect from Buffalo, New York. Church of England trends and the prevailing belief that correct church design reflected the styles of the Christian medieval age influenced Otis' design. As St. John's neared completion, one English visitor wrote of his relief that the Episcopalians of Savannah could soon abandon their Greek-inspired temple and worship in a truly proper church space.

Ironically, it is not a church but a synagogue (Temple Mickve Israel) that exhibits the most interesting interpretation of medieval-inspired forms, albeit mixed with some additional exotic decorative embellishments. Built for the third oldest Jewish congregation in America, the Gothic-inspired building includes a cruciform shape and has a curious blend of pointed arches and Middle Eastern references. The temple dates to the late 1870s; the congregation, initially a mixture

of mostly German and Portuguese refuges, dates to 1733, a reminder that many of the first individuals to settle in Savannah came from Europe in pursuit of greater religious freedom.

Savannah continued to demonstrate her reputation for religious tolerance with the establishment of new churches throughout the nineteenth century. Generally, these new congregations erected smaller, but equally charming, buildings. Often found on trust lots in the eastern and western wards of the Historic District, most of these buildings embrace Gothic Revivalism. Their Gothic undertakings and decorations were undoubtedly influenced by their budgets. On Whitefield Square, at the Congregationalist Church where missionaries worshiped with free blacks, a magnificent stained glass window dominates an otherwise plain eastern front. Nearby, on Troup Square, stands the Unitarian Church. It, too, featured Gothic detailing and an overall charming simplicity, a quality perhaps enjoyed by James Pierpont, an early choir director of Savannah's Unitarians. However, it is doubtful that the Savannah climate inspired his most famous song—"Jingle Bells."

Near the fascinating armillary sphere located in the center of Troup Square, tower the spires of Savannah's largest religious

> Wonderful and inexpensive decorative "gingerbread" contributed to the popularity of large porches and verandas for outdoor living and entertaining.

Sarah Alexander

The tower on the old jail building is a dramatic example of Savannah's attachment to the romanticism of ninteenth century architecture— in this case, the Moorish Revival Movement.

structure. Rebuilt after a fire in 1898, the Cathedral of St. John the Baptist is a fin example of late nineteenth century American Gothic Revivalism. By this time, th inspiration for many American Gothic Revivalists had veered from English pro totypes of the mid-century to those of French origin. Smaller, but not unlike S Patrick's Cathedral in New York City in profile, St. John's is filled with excep tional imported stained glass and other fine decorations reflective of its cathedra designation and the desires of its expanding congregation.

The prosperity of the nineteenth century enabled many Savannah families t become generous donors to churches as well as civic organizations. Orphanages, hos pitals, and other public institutions were the recipients of large endowments. Two o the most important institutions established in the nineteenth century are deepl indebted to the support of the Telfair family. They are the Georgia Historica Society and the Telfair Academy of Arts and Sciences. The museum is located part ly within the former residence of Mary Telfair, the daughter of the builder. Left t the Georgia Historical Society in 1875, the home was transformed into the first pub lic art museum in the South. Elements of William Jay's original design can still b seen through important restorations of two original rooms during the 1980s. Equall impressive is the exceptional collection of American impressionist paintings.

THE LADY WITH A DIRTY FACE

Even though Savannah had fallen to tenth in a census of Southern cities in 1890, i was still growing at a healthy pace and would exceed fifty-four thousand resident in 1900. The port was still actively trading, although the cotton crops were becom ing less profitable. Much of Savannah's commercial activity shifted to Broughton Street, and several skyscrapers of ten stories or more shadowed the area of Bul Street from Bay to Broughton by 1910. Streetcar travel was replaced by automo biles and buses during the years around World War I, and suburbs like Ardsle Park were developed more than a mile to the south of the Historic District.

Few Savannahians could have believed that the prosperity of the 1870s and 1880s would decline so dramatically during the early twentieth century Nonetheless, by the mid-1920s Savannah had fallen into the depths of recessior and very slow growth. With the spread of the boll weevil to Georgia during th early twentieth century, Savannah's economic base was shattered. Cotton produc tion plummeted and the significance of the port declined as manufacturing and transportation centers such as Birmingham and Atlanta emerged as the new citie of the Deep South.

Today, many citizens and visitors view this period of minimal prosperity with great sense of relief; as other American cities saw significant change, Savannah saw little. Few new buildings were erected and few existing structures were torn down. Not all of Savannah's prestigious landmarks survived; however, more often buildings were abandoned and boarded up. While the suburbs became the popular destination for new generations of old families to live, shop and work, the oldest sections of the city became increasingly derelict. During this time, Savannah entertained one of its most famous visitors, Lady Astor, who is reported to have described the city as "a beautiful lady with a dirty face."

Broughton Street, which had become Savannah's main shopping street in the nineteenth century, still served as the principal commercial district for the city through the 1960s. The African-American community generally frequented businesses along old West Broad Street (now Martin Luther King Jr. Boulevard) and photographs from the 1940s reveal a bustling downtown where ladies shopped in hats and gloves as lights, strung from one side of the street to the other, provided a delightful backdrop to the department stores, movie theaters and ice cream parlors.

Although the vibrancy and status of the city had slipped, Savannah did not venture into complete hibernation. Importantly, the recognition of Savannah's historic significance and architectural treasures had begun. More and more, citizens began to see the need to protect and preserve the beauty that had survived. Equally important, other individuals contributed positively to the community and beyond. During the first half of the twentieth century, Savannah saw several notable achievements highlighted by the establishment of the Girl Scouts of America by Savannah's Juliette Gordon Low in 1913.

Born on the eve of the Civil War, Juliette Gordon grew up in one of Savannah's finest residences. She married William Mackay Low, the son of millionaire Andrew Low, and they spent most of their married life in Britain. Here she met Sir Robert Baden-Powell, the founder of the Boy Scouts in England. Following the death of her husband, Low returned to Savannah in 1912 and resided in her former father-in-law's home on Lafayette Square until her death in 1927. In this home she founded the organization dedicated to the positive development of young women in Savannah, America and throughout the world.

The Colonial Dames of Georgia purchased the Andrew Low House shortly after the death of Juliette Gordon Low. Although the furnishings were spread among families and sold at auctions, this society was instrumental in opening the residence as Savannah's first historic house museum. Refurnished with generous donations from the membership, this museum counts some of Savannah's finest treasures among its collection.

However, it is the birthplace of Juliette "Daisy" Gordon Low that is visited by thousands each year. Maintained by the Girl Scouts of America, the residence was purchased partly by funds raised by scouts during the "Dimes for Daisy" campaign. Today it serves as an important center for the organization's programs and provides a thoughtful glimpse of late nineteenth century interior design and lifestyle.

A SAVANNAH RENAISSANCE

"The Book," as many refer to John Berendt's best-selling opus *Midnight in the Garden of Good and Evil*, has made a tremendous impact on Savannah. There is no argument that it has brought a great deal of attention (good and bad) to the city. That book, as well as movies such as *Forrest Gump*, has been partly responsible for the phenomenal rise in tourism that has taken place since the mid-nineteen nineties. But an accurate explanation for the "renaissance" we see today is more involved.

The Savannah that Berendt wrote about goes back to 1980. However, the city that caught the imagination of the public after the book was published in 1994 was vastly different. No longer sleepy, Savannah had changed dramatically.

Chang-Hyun Kim

Bright British accents—double-decker London buses—are supplied by the Savannah College of Art and Design. Oglethorpe surely would appreciate this salute to the city's origins.

A Savannah Renaissance

The initial wave of "Midnight"-inspired visitors who came to Savannah aft 1994 would have left town less enchanted if Savannah had remained as it was dur ing the early '80s. However, these tourists and travel writers arrived to find tha the Savannah of Jim Williams, Lady Chablis, and Emma Kelly was fun, fixed uj and lively. Greeting these guests were renewed residences and revitalized larg buildings, elegant eateries, sophisticated and funky shops, new bars, restaurant discotheques, and people—lots more people.

Savannah and the nation owe a great deal of gratitude to the private citizer and various organizations that have protected the visual reminders of our rich an fascinating history. From the Colonial Dames to the thoughtful and industriou Girl Scouts, our community has benefited from the hard work and contributior of hundreds of citizens. During the 1960s and 1970s, a period often described a "sleepy," the Historic Savannah Foundation and the Savannah Landmark pro grams were instrumental in saving a number of threatened residential and com mercial structures in the historic core.

The Historic Savannah Foundation was organized in 1955. The impetus grev from the desire of several Savannah women to prohibit the demolition of anothe structure of great significance: the Isaiah Davenport House. Constructed for one (the city's most successful builders, the house was completed in 1820. Most feature were reminiscent of the popular Georgian style of the eighteenth centur Although more "old-fashioned" than Jay's Regency-inspired designs, the buildin was one of Savannah's oldest surviving buildings and about to become a parking lo A tenement during much of the twentieth century, it was acquired by the newl created foundation and opened as the third historic house museum in the cit Likewise, Savannah Landmark explored innovative approaches funded by publi and private sources to reclaim areas of the Victorian District with programs tha renewed community interest in beautiful neighborhoods suffering from neglect.

Today Savannah relishes its newfound prominence and secretly enjoy finding itself on a list of the best places to visit. Some locals can be caugh whispering "kinda like Charleston"—although none would publicly admit i The city that visitors enjoy today is not a result of "The Book," but rather combination of public, private and individual initiative. First and foremost, thi "renaissance" was a result of the growth and development of the Savanna College of Art and Design.

This college was founded by Richard Rowan and Paula Rowan, May Poette and Paul Poetter to provide degree programs not previously available in south

Lin Wang

ast Georgia and to create a specialized college committed to exceptional visual arts education and effective career preparation. The college was seen as a positive addition to the community's important historically African-American college, Savannah State College (now University) and to another popular public institution, Armstrong State College (now Armstrong Atlantic State University).

In the spring of 1979, the college purchased Preston's Savannah Volunteer Guards Armory to serve as the main classroom building. Known today as Poetter Hall, the building's historic significance was recognized by its nomination for inclusion in the National Register of Historic Places.

Despite the strides made in the residential area of downtown Savannah during the 1970s and most of the 1980s, many commercial and large buildings remained vacant and neglected. The college changed this. Almost every building purchased and restored by the college had been abandoned, neglected or derelict. This still holds true today as the college continues to buy and restore buildings exhibiting various levels of disrepair. The results of over twenty years of restoration by the college in Savannah are significant and include over one million square feet of saved space without razing an existing structure or wooded area or stressing the environment. In 1994 the Savannah College of Art and Design won an Honor Award from the National Trust for Historic Preservation for preservation and adaptive use of thirty-four

Forsyth Park's magnificent fountain serves as a backdrop for many a celebration. Here students are depicted competing in the park's pinnacle event, the Savannah College of Art and Design's annual Sidewalk Arts Festival.

buildings. In the areas of art education, preservation, and urban revitalization, the college is recognized as a model for colleges and universities throughout the world.

The presence of the college throughout the historic downtown area has contributed dramatically to the community. Besides making a huge economic impact on the city, the college has been instrumental in expanding the arts scene. The college is directly involved in sponsorship of several events such as the annual Sidewalk Arts Festival, Arts on the River celebration, and the Savannah Film and Video Festival. These programs complement the prestigious Savannah Onstage music festival and the ever popular and often raucous St. Patrick's Day Parade.

THE FUTURE

The mood of the city is, once again, extremely optimistic. Savannah has had an eventful past of successes and failures that could not have been envisioned by the colonial trustees.

Savannah's fate has always been linked to commerce, hospitality and the river. As the rest of Georgia races into the countryside to make room for her unbridled growth, Savannah has taken a bold, calculated step across the river to Hutchinson Island. An outdated and undeveloped area of the port has, in the year 2000, been converted into the site of a multi-million dollar trade center and urban resort, including a luxury hotel, health spa and golf course. This new growth will strengthen the link between the river and Savannah's Historic District, the twin bonds of trade and tourism that define Savannah. Ferries carry tourists to and from each destination. From the Savannah International Trade and Convention Center on Hutchinson Island, the riverfront may be viewed in its entirety. Once again, the bluff that attracted both Oglethorpe and the Yamacraw before him has become the focal point of Savannah's future.

The Savannah Renaissance continues into the twenty-first century with the initial development of Hutchinson Island on the Savannah River, directly across from historic River Street. With this expansion, Savannah stands poised to reclaim its place as a premier American city.

Lin Wang

River Street

Lin Wang

Suspended walkways over Factors Walk enabled merchants to view and price the cotton being transported below. Now these bridges transport visitors to the activities of River Street.

"The harbour is said to be very good, & often filled with square rigged vessels but there is a bar below… rice and tobacco are the principle Exports— Lumber & Indigo are also Exported, but the latter is on the decline, and it i. supposed by Hemp & Cotton." —GEORGE WASHINGTON, 177?

Although multi-masted sailing ships have given way to tankers and container vessels larger than the first settlers could ever have imagined, River Street contains many vestiges of Savannah's port city roots. Above River Street, Oglethorpe selected Yamacraw Bluff as the site for Savannah. From here the city grew southward. Sparked by the rapid growth of the railroad by the mid-nineteenth century, the port was busy transporting cotton and other materials up the eastern seaboard and abroad. During this period, warehouses for these goods were erected with fronts feeding the schooners moored along the wharves of the river. Second fronts faced the bluff along today's Bay Street and were connected by suspended walkways, many of which are viable today.

Construction along the river continued following the Civil War as Savannah became the premier cotton port on the south Atlantic coast. During the late nineteenth century, the river of Savannah teemed with vessels of all shapes and sizes, and the new City Hall erected to replace the old exchange in 1906, symbolized the city's booming prosperity.

The warehouses of this bygone time have been rejuvenated and adapted to a new economy: the cavernous rooms of cotton bales once presented by General Sherman to President Lincoln have been replaced by shops, galleries and nightclubs. Across the river Hutchinson Island is under development. From the outdoor plaza o the new Savannah International Trade and Convention Center, visitors can enjoy a view of Savannah not unlike the one glimpsed by those arriving by ship a century earlier. The clopping hooves and grinding carriage wheels echo from the cobblestones of River Street in this timeless city, Savannah.

Millions of visitors flock to the cobblestoned River Street each year to enjoy food, shopping, music and the ambience of its rich history.

Lin Wang

Jonathan Newsome

Savannah is one of the largest container ports in the South, facilitating the passage of giant ships from all over the world. The Eugene Talmadge Bridge provides a dramatic overpass for both merchant and passenger vessels.

Christopher Hoff

The rails that feed into River Street were rarely empty a century ago, when trains were vital to Savannah's burgeoning commerce. The rattle of a lonely train can still be heard on these tracks from time to time.

Brian Main

Whether by land or water, entertainment abounds on River Street. Lively riverboat tours give passengers the opportunity to approach Savannah as many newcomers did over the last two centuries. On the sidewalks, under awnings, and in its small parks, River Street teems with live music, street artists, and the wonderful aroma of local cuisine throughout the year.

Andrew Holahan

Chang Hyun Kim

Heng-Ching Chang

Sumiyo Toribe

City Hall, crowned with a gold leaf dome,
is a reminder of Savannah's prosperity at
the turn of the century. In 1906, when
City Hall was erected, Savannah was still
one of the largest cities in the South.

Jo-Shan Ma

Along the riverfront, one can
discover secret portals and
hidden stairways that hark back
to the bustle of business long ago.

Christopher Hoff

Linda Rorer

The Savannah Cotton Exchange building was the center of cotton commerce at the turn of the century. Designed by William Gibbons Preston, the facade boasts exceptional use of terra cotta details depicting its roots in cotton.

———————

Until the early twentieth century, fleets of handsome sailing vessels reflected the prominence of Savannah's role in the booming cotton industry.

L.W. 98.   Lin Wang

Historic District

*Savannah is a favorite destination
for Girl Scouts as they pay homage
to their founder, Savannahian
Juliette Gordon Low.*

First impressions can be deceiving. T
pristine white columns, pink and g
bricks, and lush green grass m
resemble more an idyll than a mod
American city. But the Histo
District of Savannah is vibrantly, p
pably real. These two square m
marry reminders of a rich and colorful past with
emergence of a spirited community ignited by prospe
for the new century. True to her history, Savannah
adapting to the challenges and opportunities of the futu
without compromising the lessons learned from her pa

Savannah boasts some of the loveliest buildings in
United States, complemented by a lush backdrop of tre
moss, and flowers throughout the year. Elegant shad
streets and avenues are portals to architectural treasu
but most significant to Savannah's distinct charm are
city squares. These green oases beg travelers to linger a
soak up the rich ambience. In early spring, azaleas a
daffodils paint the parks in pas
hues; in early summer, fragr
jasmine and magnolia embell
the squares' monuments, fou
tains, and historical markers. Even
winter, camellias and pansies
reminders of Savannah's perpetual
Whether walking, biking or driving,
city squares require visitors to slow do

Wempy Homeric

nd smell the roses.

Inquirers find that most residents ave a favorite square—the choice elying on a variety of factors, mpulses and personal experiences. Whitefield Square's charming gaze-o is a popular spot for staging pringtime weddings amid the looming forsythia and dogwood, nd nearby Calhoun Square recalls avannah before 1900, as all the uildings date prior to this time. Chippewa Square was the setting for orrest Gump's bus stop (alas, it was ut a prop), and among the mansion-ned sidewalks of Monterey Square the now famous Mercer House, ormer residence of Jim Williams nd setting for John Berendt's best-eller, *Midnight in the Garden of Good and Evil*. Oglethorpe's original lans for clear, open spaces have volved into mini-forests. In Madison quare, glimpses of cornices and olumns, steeples and chimneys are evealed in fragments through the entury-old live oaks and dangling noss.

Designing a tour of the historic istrict is next to impossible, with isitors lured in different directions. Not to worry. Savannah seduces you, naring all her charms in due time.

L.W.

Lin Wang

A walk through the Historic District showcases some of America's most beautiful houses of worship. German immigrants were the founders of Savannah's Lutheran Church of the Ascension.

True
afficionados
and weekend treasure
hunters delight in the many
antique shops and markets in the historic area. Jere's
Antiques displays an amazing array of objects from the past.

Lin Wang

Savannah's new City Market was built adjacent to the site of its predecessor, which was torn down to make way for a parking garage in the 1950s.

Sarah Alexander

Jon Wink

Today, the area is filled with activity. A pedestrian plaza, alfresco dining, carriage rides, artist studios, tandem bike rentals, ice cream shops, and live music create a romantic, bustling ambience.

Sumiyo Toribe

Heng-Ching Chang

Whether it's frankfurters or fettuccine, a cold beer or a young Beaujolais, you'll find what you crave just around the corner.

From former warehouses to fresh fish markets, Savannah restaurateurs treat their spaces as creatively as their cuisine. Most of the dining establishments in the Historic District are housed in buildings with a four-course past!

Heng Ching Chang

Heng-Ching Chang

Anyone seen "The King" lately?
(All the cool people stop by Velvet Elvis,
one of many hopping nightclubs
in City Market.)

Formerly the Citizens Bank, Propes Hall was the first building in Savannah to be completely fireproofed. It is now an administration building for the Savannah College of Art and Design.

Lin Wang

Dana Sink

Broughton Street was the commercial and social hub from the late nineteenth century through the 1950s, hosting theaters, department stores and fancy restaurants. Like so many downtown districts across America, Broughton Street faced great economic decline with the advent of shopping centers and malls. Its original splendor is gradually being restored, in part by efforts of the Savannah College of Art and Design.

The former Weis Theater, left abandoned until the mid-'90s, has been transformed into Trustees Theater, a resplendent art deco-style space hosting live performances throughout the year. Tony Bennett performed opening night, May 9, 1998.

Sarah Alexander

Maas Brothers, one of Broughton Street's last department stores, is well-remembered by the city's older residents. Hats and hangers have been replaced by books and computers in a state-of-the-art library designed by the Savannah College of Art and Design. Located directly across from Trustees Theater, the Jen Library is a stunning example of adaptive rehabilitation.

Though five-and-dimes are retiring, their architectural legacy continues as new businesses adopt old buildings like Kress and Woolworth's. Savannah does not adhere to the urban trend of "new is better."

Brian Main

The Talmadge Bridge is the gateway between Savannah and nearby
Hilton Head Island and Beaufort, South Carolina.

Chang-Hyun Kim

This charming cottage on Oglethorpe Avenue provides insight into the city's colonial architecture.

Sandra Reed

Many of the houses, like this modest cottage, were moved and preserved in the vicinity of Warren Square.

Erected for a single family in the late nineteenth century, the Kehoe House has been transformed into one of Savannah's most gracious inns. Much of the external embellishments are rendered in cast iron, as the Kehoe family owned the local ironworks.

Many visitors to Savannah enjoy the alternative accommodations provided by such intimate inns.

Lin Wang

L.W. 98.

A bird's-eye view of Madison Square portrays a skyline largely unchanged for more than a century.

Dana Sink

The spire of Independent Presbyterian Church seems to glow against rainy skies. A favorite reference point for travelers along Bull Street, the church is one of many architectural delights stretching from the river to Forsyth Park.

Christopher Hoff

49

John Holden Greene's Independent Presbyterian Church was inspired by the church architecture of eighteenth century London. Dedicated in 1819, the original church was rebuilt following the devastating fire of 1889.

Lin Wang

In 1853, architect John S. Norris built the city's most expensive house, and one of the South's finest examples of Gothic Revivalism. The Green-Meldrim house sheltered Union General William Tecumseh Sherman during his infamous march into Savannah.

Lin Wang

The Massie Heritage Interpretation Center was dedicated for the education of poor children, and is the only remaining building of Georgia's original chartered school system. Today it houses permanent exhibits that highlight the history, city plan and preservation efforts of the community.

Lin Wang

Looming above Wright Square, this tower is inspired by the campanili of Italy.

Andrew Holahan

Supposedly built over the objections of the family, the William Washington Gordon monument commemorates a founder of the Central of Georgia Railroad and dominates the center of Wright Square. Nearby, one can find the monument to Yamacraw chieftain Tomochichi, who welcomed the first colonists.

Built in 1906, the Scottish Rite building is considered Savannah's most entertaining and magnificent example of Beaux-Arts-inspired classicism.

Lin Wang

Lin Wang

Bay windows and awnings often define entrances to popular neighborhood restaurants, like this cafe on Troup Square.

Brian Mai

Heng-Ching Chang

President Monroe attended a lavish reception at the Scarbrough House, one of the three surviving mansions designed by William Jay. Restored by the Historic Savannah Foundation in the 1970s, today it houses the venerable Ships of the Sea Museum. Fittingly, William Scarbrough was a principal financier of the S.S. Savannah, the first steam-powered vessel to cross the Atlantic Ocean.

Wempy Homeric

One of Savannah's great Greek Revival townhomes, the Sorrel-Weed mansion, has a vivid pumpkin hue. Designed by Charles Cluskey in 1841, the Sorrel-Weed home, like many formidable dwellings in Savannah, is still privately owned.

Charul Sakultanapaisal

Savannah's late, great nineteenth century hotel, the DeSoto, was an extravagant Romanesque Revival structure. Decorative details of this former grand dame, which was torn down in the 1960s, survive in selected buildings throughout the city.

A resemblance to the former DeSoto Ho~~t~~ may be seen in the details of Poetter H~~a~~ (formerly the Savannah Volunteer Gua~~rd~~ Armory). Both buildings were designed ~~by~~ William Gibbons Preston.

Charul Sakultanapaisal

The concentration of so many nineteenth and early
twentieth century buildings of distinction makes
Savannah a subject for study by architectural
historians from all over the world.

Andrew Holahan

A pint at the Six Pence Pub is one of many ways to unwind in Savannah.

Wempy Homeric

Savannah encourages walking. New pleasures are revealed on even the most familiar path, from details in wrought iron to autumn light falling through hanging moss. It is little wonder that artists linger here.

Jo-Shan Ma

Lin Wang

Savannah's renaissance has been ignited by the growth of the Savannah College of Art and Design, which began in the former Savannah Volunteer Guards Armory. Established in 1979, the college has grown from its original class of 71 to nearly 5,000 aspiring artists from all over the world. Renamed Poetter Hall, this flagship building now houses two galleries, classrooms, and the college's award-winning printing department.

Across the street from Poetter Hall, students and visitors alike enjoy high tea, Savannah-style, at the college's Gryphon Tea Room.

Wempy Homeric

A former post office, built in 1898 by architect William Aiken, this building was more than doubled in size in 1931 by James A. Westmore. The newer section was seamlessly integrated into the old, resulting in one of Savannah's most timeless works of architecture.

Lin Wang

Chang-Hyun K.

The annual St. Patrick's Day Parade is reported to be the second largest in the country, attracting hundreds of thousands to the city each year.

Some of the Historic District's most delightful and tranquil private gardens are visible along Jones Street.

Gothic and Moorish features of Temple Mickve Israel combine to create one of the most beautiful synagogues in America.

Chang-Hyun Kim

Chang-Hyun Kim

Lin Wang

The upper floor of the Wayne-Gordon House was added at the time of the marriage of Juliette Gordon to William Mackay Low in 1886. Juliette Gordon Low founded the Girl Scouts of America in Savannah in 1912.

Jo-Shan Ma

The Armstrong mansion, designed by Henrik Wallin, was considered the city's grandest home in the early 1900s. This Beaux-Arts showpiece was featured in the 1919 issue of "American Architect."

Colonial Park Cemetery was used for burials until the early nineteenth century. A bucolic green space housing a fascinating array of tombs and monuments, the cemetery is the resting place of many of Savannah's earliest settlers and prominent citizens. Button Gwinnett, a signer of the Declaration of Independence, is buried here.

Jon Wink

Victorian-era graveyards:
Laurel Grove and Bonaventure.

Charul Sakultanapaisa

Heng-Ching Chang

Lin Wang

Many see the Cathedral of St. John the Baptist as the crown jewel of Savannah's religious architecture. The monochromatic exterior gives way to a frenzy of colorful decoration inside.

Members of the Savannah Ladies' Memorial Association—forerunner of the present United Daughters of the Confederacy—dedicated this monument in Forsyth Park.

Andrew Holahan

Charul Sakultanapaisal

Andrew Holahan

Stephen Johnson

Jonathan Newsome

Look closely as you travel along the streets and through the squares of Savannah. There is always something new to discover in the faces of the buildings, tombstones, fountains and portals. Delight in the stories these details share!

Stephen Johnson

Jonathan Newsome

Different builders and tastes are reflected in the diverse materials of stucco, brick and wood used on the exterior of these Charlton Street homes.

Andrew Holahan

James Habersham Jr. built this home in 1789. It is the most significant eighteenth century structure to survive in the city. The Olde Pink House Restaurant, which houses the oldest pub in Georgia, is a favorite haunt of locals and visitors—and a legendary ghost.

Stephen Johnson

Flannery O'Connor grew up in this house on East Charlton Street. Weekly literary readings are now held in this museum home.

Granite Steps, one of the city's great residences, recently was converted to an inn. On arrival, guests ascend one of Savannah's most beautiful external staircases.

Chang-Hyun Kim

The Central of Georgia Railroad supplied the po
with boatloads of cotton, pine and other princip
exports of the city.

Although the beautiful Central of Georgia stati
has been razed, this area boasts one of the countr

Ex Libris, a former dry goods store renovated by the
Savannah College of Art and Design, houses textbooks, art
supplies, gifts, a public gallery and a coffee bar. An excel-
lent example of the revival movement on Martin Luther
King Jr. Boulevard, Ex Libris is located across from the
former Central of Georgia Railroad complex.

Lin Wang

Brian Main

most significant extant railroad complexes. Since
1990, the Savannah College of Art and Design
has renovated several of these structures, including
Kiah Hall (above).

In 1996, the former Guaranty Life building was
re-opened as the Ralph Mark Gilbert Civil Rights
Museum, the vision of venerable historian and Civil
Rights activist W.W. Law. This interactive state-of-
the-art museum recounts Savannah citizens'
struggles and victories during the Civil Rights era.

Chang-Hyun Kim

The first church on this site (now the site of First Bryan Baptist Church) dates from 1794, and may be the oldest property in the United States owned continually by African-Americans.

Although travelers no longer ride the rail, these tracks continue to transport goods to major industrial sites in and around Savannah. Many citizens dream of the return of a passenger rail network connecting Georgia's original city with its capital, Atlanta.

Chang-Hyun Kim

Victorian District and Beyond

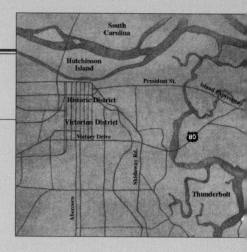

Jo-Shan Ma

Elizabeth on 37th is recognized as one of America's preeminent restaurants, attracting diners from around the world. This elegant building was built as a single-family home at the turn of the century.

"I recall my fleeting instants of Savannah as the taste of a cup charged t the brim." —HENRY JAMES, 1907

Forsyth Park is a lovely preface to the Victoria District. A truly marvelous space, this park cover some thirty acres and is the setting for numerou festivals and activities. On the first days of sprin families may be seen picnicking and student painting, while Frisbees are tossed overhead Laughter of children on the swing sets compete with the music of a boom box or two.

Officially, the Victorian District begins and the Historic Distric ends at Gwinnett Street, although local tradition marks Gaston as th borderline crossing. An area of immense beauty and diverse commu nities, this neighborhood enjoys a resurgence of preservation activit and investment.

It was along the fringes of these districts where many members the city's African-American community lived after the Civil War. O the eastern edge of the Victorian District is the Beach Institute neigh borhood. Home to the first school for Savannah's black population this building now serves as a cultural and artistic center highlightin African-American contributions.

The history of Savannah's African-American community is sti incomplete. Creating an accurate portrait of the role played by slave and free blacks in the city's story continues to encourage researc directed by many notable individuals affiliated with outstandin organizations. These include the King-Tisdell Cottage Foundatio and the Ralph Mark Gilbert Civil Rights Museum.

Threatened with demolition in the 1970s, the King-Tisdell Cottage is considered one of Savannah's finest examples of the "gingerbread" style.

This decorative treatment was popular in the late nineteenth century and is reflected on homes throughout the Victorian District.

Wempy Homerie

Lin Wang

Beautiful and inviting Forsyth Park is Savannah's green centerpiece. This elegant fountain dates to the 1850s and is inspired by an earlier French work. It is probably the most popular backdrop for photographers, and is the site of many celebrations. Nearly thirty acres, the park was once the parade ground of the Savannah militia.

Sumiyo Toribe

The park's playground is frequently filled with children and their laughter.

Heng-Ching Chang

Heng-Ching Chang

Hall Street boasts some of the city's finest examples of Queen Anne architectural styles. The towers and turrets of the Baldwin house rise from the romantic landscape like a castle, while statues gaze dreamily from the garden next door.

Along Whitaker Street, handsome homes reveal themselves through the trees and hanging moss of Forsyth Park.

Lin Wang

As the city expanded southward in the twentieth century, developers continued to recognize the value of green spaces. These parks complement the beloved churches, stately residences, and charming bungalows found in these neighborhoods.

Grand porticoes and front porches illustrate Savannah's interest in reviving the spirit of antebellum architecture. Many a lemonade or mint julep has been sipped in the afternoon sun on these grand porches. Just south of Victory Drive may be seen wonderful examples along Atlantic and Washington avenues.

Brian Main

Savannah takes pride in its preservation efforts, which
are enjoying unprecedented activity at the turn of the
new century. Indeed, since this rendering, this large
home has been lovingly restored.

Jonathan Newsome

For a period of time, the Victorian District—so named because of its late nineteenth century architecture—was largely neglected, and once-beautiful houses were carved into apartments. However, public and private initiatives have begun to creatively restore and revive historic structures, which make up some of the most livable and eclectic neighborhoods in Savannah.

Sandra Reed

Jonathan Newsome

Jon Wink

Chang-Hyun Kim

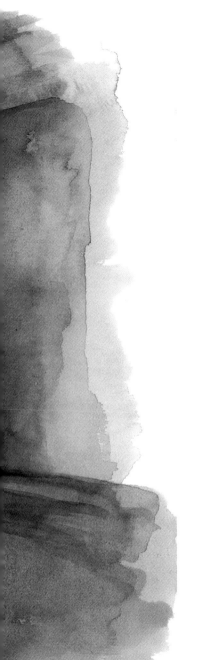

Chang-Hyun Kim

The lanes of the Victorian District have a personality different from those found in the historic core of the city.

Along Thirty-seventh Street are reminders of Savannah's suburban growth. Today, Thirty-seventh Street is a lively thoroughfare between the east and west sides of the city, hosting antique shops, restaurants, car washes, and private homes.

Robin Reynolds

As a gesture to the neighborhood and as a place for students to gather, the Savannah College of Art and Design relocated two vintage diners from out-of-state to the Victorian District. For these efforts, the college was recognized by the Art Deco Societies of America.

Chang-Hyun Kim

In the late 1980s, the flourishing Savannah College of Art and Design was seeking fresh sites for classrooms and studios, and identified the Victorian District as a prime location. Several former school buildings, such as Henry Hall, were revived for their original purpose—education. During the following decade, the presence of college activity has led to further private investment and restoration in the district. Meanwhile, the international assimilation of art students into the neighborhood has served as a catalyst for renewed vigor and diversity.

Chang-Hyun Kim

Islands and Beaches

The Rails to Trails
nature walk near Talahi
Island is a bird-watcher's
paradise.

Sandra Reed

The landscape surrounding Savannah remind us that the river was aptly named. A Oglethorpe sailed upstream he viewed mile of flat and largely treeless expanses reminis cent of an African savanna. Fishing village and plantations were often established, a Savannah was, on sandy bluffs adjacent t navigable waterways. Thunderbolt and Wormsloe are notabl examples. Undoubtedly the bewitching romance of these coasta communities enchanted the early colonists and inspired Johnn Mercer to write the immortal lyrics to "Moon River." Sunset spied along the river's banks or through the live oaks and mon uments of Bonaventure cemetery continue to dazzle and deligh

Here, too, you can enjoy a variety of lifestyles. From the care fully planned and manicured communities of Skidaway Island t the eclectic mix of old and new on Isle of Hope, the suburban area of Savannah have their own unique personalities. The relaxe decorum of Tybee Island, for example, would not be confused wit the sensibilities of her neighbor, Hilton Head, where more feet ar shod in golf shoes than sand. But whether you prefer to be well heeled or bare-heeled, visitors find a style to suit them.

Lin Wang

Walkways provide access to the beach and protect the fragile dunes
that buffer beachfront homes from the constant lapping of the Atlantic.

Heng-Ching Chang

ebuilt in 1996, many years
fter a devastating fire, the
ybrisa Pier renews the spirit
f the original, which was
he site of countless galas
nd dances in the first half
f the century. Today, as in
he past, it attracts anglers
nd party-goers alike.

Fort Screven and Tybee Lighthouse
anchor the north end of the island. One
of America's oldest and finest examples of
lighthouse architecture, this beacon has
guided thousands of sailors to safety for
over two hundred years.

Wempy Homeric

Locals and tourists flock to
the inimitable Crab Shack,
home to seafood, beer and
beautiful marsh sunsets.
Shoes are optional.

Wempy Homeric

Whether shopping or
dining, the style is distinctly
casual on Tybee, an island that hosts
the annual Beach Bums parade.

Brian Main

Chang-Hyun Kim

Fort Pulaski's imposing brick walls were begun in 1829 and finished in the 1840's. Considered by General Robert E. Lee to be impenetrable, these seven-foot-thick walls were pierced after thirty hours of attack by Union forces in the Civil War. Today, it is a national monument with five hundred thirty-seven surrounding acres home to native wildlife.

Farther upriver is a second stronghold, Fort Jackson. Like so many of Savannah's monuments, these forts inspire imaginations of another age.

Stephen Johnson

Island homes are often graced by sweeping lawns and ancient oaks, harking back to long-ago lazy afternoons of croquet and social banter.

Boating is a way of life on the islands, where fishing and recreational outings are popular in all seasons. The waters of the Atlantic and surrounding creeks abound with marine life, including friendly (and curious!) dolphins.

Heng-Ching Chang

Linda Rorer

The beach transforms into a playground at low tide for cyclists, joggers and shell hunters.

The muted colors of the rivers and surrounding marshes change subtly with each season. Across the bridge from Garden City and only minutes away from downtown, the Savannah Wildlife Refuge is home to indigenous creatures large and small, including egrets, cranes, blue herons, osprey, box turtles, raccoons, snakes, and, of course, alligators! On a spring day, one can view multiple gators basking in the sun.

Andrew Holahan

Beach houses are often colorful, charming, but above all, practical. Most dwellings on Tybee are built on stilts to withstand floods from Atlantic storms. Weather is heeded seriously by beach dwellers, particularly during the early autumn months known as hurricane season.

Robin Reynolds

Historic Isle of Hope is only minutes from the city. Along the banks of the Skidaway River, this village has evolved from a pastoral summer retreat of the nineteenth century into a close-knit neighborhood of exquisite homes, magnificent oaks, and sunsets that are free to all.

Jon Wink

Pinpoint, Georgia, was the birthplace of Supreme Court Justice Clarence Thomas.

Chang-Hyun Kim

Chang-Hyun Kim

Heng-Ching Chang

Thunderbolt, established in 1739 as a defensive bastion for Savannah's eastern flank, is a thriving community of fishermen, boat builders, artists and entrepreneurs. Nearby, Savannah State University was originally established in 1890 as one of the first institutions in the South to offer higher education to African-Americans.

Tybee Lighthouse today resembles nothing of the wooden tower built shortly after Oglethorpe established the colony.

The Atlantic Intercoastal Waterway winds along Savannah's Wilmington and Skidaway rivers. The southeast seaboard is filled with fishing boats, pleasure boats, yachts, and the occasional jet ski. The legendary patience of Savannah residents is in part inspired by long waits at the drawbridge!

Heng-Ching Chang

Stephen Johnson

Visitors to Wormsloe are greeted with a dramatic canopy of live oaks, whose twisting limbs provide a grand entrance to the old plantation, lately a popular site for Hollywood films.

Linda Rorer

At Wormsloe, tabby ruins provide a glimpse into the culture and operation of the first fortified plantation in Georgia.

Port Wentworth has developed responsible growth patterns for the future as it respects and preserves its many pockets of natural beauty. Fishing on the marshes here is a popular pastime.

Of Bonaventure Cemetery John Muir once said, "If that burying ground across the Sea of Galilee, mentioned in Scripture, was half as beautiful as Bonaventure, I do not wonder that a man should dwell among the tombs.

Still in operation today, the Bethesda Home For Boys was established in 1740 under the direction of colonist James Habersham and Pastor George Whitefield. The chapel is one of the loveliest buildings on the grounds, and is a popular site for weddings.

Sarah Alexander

Jonathan Newsome

J.N.
'98

Selected Reading and Sources For Further Learning

Allen, Patrick (ed.), *Literary Savannah*. Athens: Hill Street Press, 1999

Johnson, Whittington B., *Black Savannah 1788-1864*. Little Rock: University of Arkansas Press, 1999

Lane, Mills, *Savannah Revisited: History and Architecture*. Savannah: Beehive Press, 1994

Russell, Preston and Barbara Hines, *Savannah: A History of Her People Since 1733*. Savannah: Frederic C. Beil, 1993

Talbott, Page and Daniel L. Grantham, *Classical Savannah: Fine and Decorative Arts 1800 - 1840*. Athens: University of Georgia Press, 1995

Toledano, Roulhac, *The National Trust Guide to Savannah: Architectural and Cultural Treasures*. New York: John Wiley & Sons, 1997

Wittish, Rich, *The Insiders' Guide to Savannah*. Helena: Insiders' Publishing Inc., 1999

The Georgia Historical Society, 501 Whitaker Street, Savannah, Georgia 31401

Historic Savannah Foundation, 321 East York Street, Savannah, Georgia 31401

Juliette Gordon Low Girl Scout National Center, 142 Bull Street, Savannah, Georgia 31401

Telfair Museum of Art, 121 Barnard Street, Savannah, Georgia 31401

Beach Institute African-American Cultural Center, 502 East Harris Street, Savannah, Georgia 31401

Ralph Mark Gilbert Civil Rights Museum, 460 Martin Luther King, Jr. Blvd, Savannah, Georgia 31401

Savannah Area Chamber of Commerce, 301 Martin Luther King Jr. Blvd, Savannah, Georgia 31401